ELLIOT PAGE

The Biography of Elliot Page

University Press

D1716760

CONTENTS

INTRODUCTION

For over a decade, Christopher Nolan movies have received praise and accolades from critics and audiences. The depth in the stories and the intriguing and complex characters made him a director many actors wanted to work with for at least one movie. He grabbed attention with the unique story in Memento in 2000, and then he worked on several other well-received movies, particularly The Prestige and The Dark Knight. Finally, in 2010, he was able to work on another indie film (he was still working on the final installment of his Batman trilogy) called Inception. The cast was full of both high-profile and up-and-coming actors. One of the most promising actors was Ellen Page, someone who gained a lot of attention following the release of the indie film Juno in 2007.

Inception was rich in plot and character development, mostly led by a male cast. The only two notable women in the film were Ellen Page and Marion Cotillard, both playing vital roles. There is a very different expectation for women at premieres and on red carpets, with significant pressure to present themselves in a certain way, to embody a type of femininity that aligns with whatever the current standards in beauty are in society. There was an extra layer of stress for the young Page – he did not identify with the gender assigned to him at birth.

He best explained his feelings during an interview with Oprah in 2021: "There was so much press and so many premieres all around the world and I was wearing dresses and heels to pretty much every single event." What should have been a great career experience became more of an anxiety-driven nightmare. While preparing for a premiere in Paris, his manager brought three dresses and offered to let Page choose the one he liked most. In response, Page reported, "I lost it. It was like a cinematic moment. That night, after the premiere at the after-party, I collapsed. That's something that's happened frequently in my life, usually corresponding with a panic attack."

This did not happen due to a grueling schedule but resulted from a lifetime of societal pressures. Page said it best, "… it's every experience you've had since you were a toddler, people saying, The way you're sitting is not ladylike, you're walking like a boy. The music you're listening to as a teenager,' obviously, the way you dress. Every single aspect of who you are constantly being looked at and put in a box in a very binary system. That's what it leads to."

In that one night, his past and his future seemed to collide. In his past was a successful career as a promising actor in a highly competitive field; in his future was shedding the expectations based on a gender with which he did not identify and working to continue to live in a way more authentic to who he felt he was.

CHAPTER 1

Early Life

Born in Halifax, Canada, on February 21, 1987, to Martha Phillpotts and Dennis Page, Page was initially named Ellen Page. Halifax is a city in the province of Nova Scotia. The official language in the province is English, but there are a number of French speakers in the region because of its close proximity to Quebec. Quebec has a large population of people who speak French, and the province has both English and French as the official languages.

Phillpotts was a French teacher at one of the schools. Page's father was a graphic designer. Between the two of them, the family lived comfortably.

Nova Scotia is just north of the American state of Maine, and there are similarities between the two areas. However, most people living in Nova Scotia and Maine live further apart, making it more likely that people there have more remote lives. As a result, Page lived a much more independent childhood than children in more urban areas.

From an early age, Page was more interested in being active instead of focusing on normal activities for girls, especially in the 20th century. Among the activities that the future actor enjoyed were biking, swimming, and playing soccer. Later he would make it clear that he enjoyed being outside, especially in such a gorgeous part of North America; "You're just surrounded by so much beauty and stillness."

Page may have wanted to escape from home because his parents divorced while Page was still young. Following the divorce, Page moved between two homes to meet the custody agreement requirements. This meant living in a different home every two weeks. While the divorce did seem amicable, the constant movement may have left him feeling less settled. His mother's family lived in Toronto, Canada, so Page often joined his mother on trips to visit the maternal side of the family. Even though he grew up in a quieter area, the visits to Toronto gave the young Page a taste of living in a major city. Part of this included seeing shows and enjoying the kinds of entertainment only available in larger urban areas. This included one visit to a theater to watch *The Phantom of the Opera* live, an experience that stuck with the young Page in a way that influenced his future career path. Years later, Page remembered the magical experience and wanted to pursue acting as a career. As the play ended, Page wanted to play the role of Christine, the main female character in the play. This does demonstrate that at the time, Page was listening to what others said and was trying to fit into an outside perception of what he should be, asking specifically about acting as the female. However, Christine is admittedly one of the toughest characters to play in a musical because of the large singing range required to play the character. Lord Andrew Lloyd Webber wrote the role for his then-wife, Sarah Brightman, who has an impressive three-octave range. This could have also been the draw, as the character has more time on stage than any other character, including the titular Phantom.

Whatever drew Page to the play was a turning point in the youngster's life. Not even ten years old, he decided to be an actor. His mother told him that to get a role like that, Page would need to go to college, helping the young child start mapping out a future of what was required to reach a goal quickly forming in his head.

CHAPTER 2

Acting

U nlike many people, Page decided to pursue a career in acting and then did not stray from that path. While most people tend to dream and hope that things will work out, Page began getting into the types of activities that would more easily translate into a successful acting career. Even though his mother had said he could go into acting after college, Page wasn't willing to wait until he was older before working toward his goal. His school had a drama club that helped teach the youngster necessary tasks and exercises that helped improve one's chances of advancing in acting. The club was adept at teaching some of the basics kids need to know, but Page also clearly had a lot of natural talent to draw from, even in those early days.

In 1997 at ten years old, Page earned his first acting role in a made-for-TV movie called *Pit Pony*.

Reflecting much later in his life, Page said, "It's just mind-boggling, what I do now. I sometimes think, "what if I was sick that day the casting guy came into the school?" It shows an awareness of how fortunate he was to have that early opportunity, and demonstrates how luck is just as important as skill when it comes to a career like acting. Being in the right place at the right time has been instrumental to many people who have found success in the industry. In Page's case, so many things could have resulted in someone else getting the role. He had to be in the right place at the right time. Considering he lived in a remote location, the odds were already low that he would be the person chosen for the part. In some measure, the school's club was part of why he even had the opportunity – it was the reason that a casting director came to the school in the first place. If Page hadn't joined the club or had been absent for any reason that day, it's possible that his life would have been very different.

Instead, Page was hired to take on a role in a movie that soon became a TV series, giving the youngster a much better chance of success in an incredibly difficult industry. With this opportunity, Page ensured it was impossible to miss just how much he brought to the craft, even when he was still very young.

The movie is about a boy named Willie MacLean who lived in Nova Scotia in 1901. After his older brother is killed and his father seriously injured in the collapse of a mine. Willie takes a job working in the mine to support his family. It is meant to be a temporary job while his father recovers from his injury. He ends up working with one of the ponies in the pit, and they develop a bond. Page played one of his younger sisters, who he was trying to support in his work. It isn't exactly a feel-good movie, meaning the children who played the younger roles had to be able to sell some very difficult emotions. Given the hard subject matter and the age of several actors, the movie gained much attention at the Canadian Gemini Awards, which recognized Canadian actors between 1986 and 2011. Though not nominated for an award, the movie getting a lot of attention helped Page gain some notice. It also allowed the movie to be picked up and turned into a short-running series. He was again cast to play the role of one of the younger sisters from 1999 to 2000.

With his foot in the door and a role with some meat already under his belt, he continued to find more work in Canadian TV. Finally, despite being young, he was cast in a movie filmed for a European movie. This was the first taste of real independence that most people don't experience until much later in life, largely because his parents had full-time jobs that kept them too busy for all the management required for a child to be an actor. This didn't mean he had to do everything alone, but Page was more responsible for his career path than many other children his age. The biggest hurdle was that children were required to have an adult on set with them. Since his parents couldn't be on set, they had to find another solution. Page later said, "We'd finagle it so, say, the horse-wrangler's daughter was my chaperone," showing that even before he was an adult, he was able to ensure that all of the requirements were met so that he could continue to pursue his chosen career. Given how skilled he is, it is a good thing that the studio was willing to work around the more complicated life that he led and his familial limitations.

With a fairly robust career already under his belt, Page decided that the best career move at just 16 years old was to relocate to Toronto. There were more opportunities there than in his hometown. However, he didn't remain there for very long before an opportunity arose for him to move somewhere that gave him the biggest opportunity to thrive as an actor – he moved to California to act in an American movie.

CHAPTER 3

Rising Star

There are many movie markets worldwide, but Hollywood is still where most actors want to go to make it as a film star. Page made the trek to the notoriously difficult location for actors at just 16 years old. Armed with a couple of roles in serious parts, he got the difficult role of Hayley Stark in the movie Hard Candy. The character is a 14-year-old who is on the cheerleading team, and she has been flirting with a man online. One day she agrees to meet the man, Jeff Kohlver, at a coffeehouse to talk. He is 32, making him nearly twice her age. However, the movie isn't quite what a casual viewer may expect – the girl isn't the victim she appears to be.

The audience's apprehension is palpable when Jeff invites her back to his house. Given their online flirtations, it is difficult not to expect that he is planning on pushing for more contact, and this suspicion is heightened when he makes them both a drink and offers one to her. Hayley turns down the drink, stating that she was taught not to accept drinks she hadn't made herself. She goes into his kitchen to make a replacement pair of drinks. The pair walk around his home, with the camera making it clear that Hayley is noting the pictures of scantily clad girls around her age located around his home. Inspired by the pictures, she requests that he take her picture, so when he goes to get his camera, it feels as if she is about to become a victim. As she starts posing for him, though, Jeff passes out. Upon waking up, he quickly becomes aware that he is tied up and unable to move. Hayley has tied him up to one of his own chairs. When she knows that he's awake, the main character begins to explain that she believes he is a sexual predator, using the fact that he brought her to his house after flirting with her online as a way of proving that she is right in her assumption. Jeff denies having done anything she accuses him of doing, but Hayley does not believe him. After searching through his house, she finds potential evidence that he is connected to one of the local disappearances, then he attacks her. Following a short struggle, she manages to get the better of him, again knocking him unconscious. This time when he wakes up, she has him tied down to a metal table, and it is clear what she plans to do. Disbelieving his declarations of innocence, she plans to torture him. With a medical book, she begins the torture.

The main character is dark and adept at mind games, so it is interesting to watch how a young girl can interact with someone much older and stronger than her. There is no real resolution or answer, but the movie does end with some indications of whether or not he is guilty.

Not an easy watch, the movie was first shown at the Sundance Film Festival in 2005, giving it an audience that was more likely able to handle the darker subject matter. It was again shown at a festival the next year, this time the Florida Film Festival. Following the second festival, it was given an incredibly limited release, appearing only in two theaters in the US, one in LA and the other in New York City. It was then released on a larger scale, earning over $8 million internationally.

The movie received some critical praise, with critics noting that the dark subject matter can be difficult viewing, but that Page was outstanding in the lead role. However, it was clear that the movie was not for everyone, with the movie getting 67% on Rotten Tomatoes and 58% based on reviews conducted by Metacritic. The renowned critic Roger Ebert went on to give the film 3.5/4 stars, describing the movie as follows: "There is undeniable fascination in the situation as it unfolds...., *Hard Candy* is impressive and effective." Many reviewers specifically called out Page and the actor who played Jeff, Patrick Wilson, for their strong performances, regardless of how someone feels about the movie.

Naturally, people compared the red hoodie that Page's character wore to Little Red Riding Hood, further making the audience feel that she is the innocent victim who is likely too naïve to succeed in protecting herself. While this is probably something that does affect the way people perceive the character, especially given Page's more innocent portrayal of the character, except at key moments when she shows her true colors against the perceived predator. Unfortunately, this was not a conscious choice by the people behind the scenes. They didn't make the connection until other people did, making it a fortunate coincidence that there was that kind of association.

When asked about the role, Page told a member of *The Guardian*, "Yeah, Hard Candy was intense. My dad came with me to that. But they were always cool with the subject matter, they trusted me." This was surprising considering what happens in some of the scenes, and though Page wasn't 14, she was still not legally an adult. Of course, there is a difference between the mind of a 14-year-old and a 16-year-old, but it's still a very rough topic for someone so young. When asked about that, he replied, "I remember getting ready for those scenes, I was 16, and I was almost separate from myself: shocked by it, and curious, and excited. It was a very exhilarating feeling, and very addictive.

His abilities did not go unnoticed, and *Hard Candy* is often considered his breakout role, at least in the US. However, this was the break he needed to start moving on to other roles that launched Page into celebrity status.

CHAPTER 4

Juno

As more people were recognizing his skills and abilities, Page was sent more scripts to see if they might be a good fit for his career path. When he received Juno, it seemed that Page had the same reaction to it that he had to the role of Christine in Phantom of the Opera – he knew that he wanted to become the titular teenage girl. He once told a reporter, "When I read the script it just blew my mind and I fell totally in love with it and I just really wanted to be a part of it." Though the movie does have another heavy subject matter, it doesn't have the same darkness and heft as Hard Candy. Instead, it is more of a coming of age under very difficult circumstances. Page has said of the role of the main character, "I was excited about this character because I felt like it was a teenage female lead that we've just never seen before. Although she was incredibly unique and witty and all of these things, she was also very genuine and it all felt just very sincere." It was a fantastic turn of events for Jason Reitman, the film's director, who had always imagined her in the role.

Released in 2007, *Juno* is about a 16-year-old girl named Juno MacGuff, who finds herself pregnant by one of her friends, Paulie Bleeker, played by Michael Cera (who was better known because of his role on the TV show *Arrested Development*). When she tells him that she is pregnant, she says that she plans to get an abortion, to which he says he supports any decision she makes. Arriving at a clinic, Juno finds she can't go through with it. Still, she knows she isn't ready to take care of the baby, so she decides her best option is to give the child up for adoption. She and one of her good friends, Leah, search for a couple they think will be a pair to take on the role of parents. When she meets a couple, played by Jennifer Garner and Jason Bateman (who were both much better-known actors than the younger stars), she feels they are the right couple for the role. She continues to visit them over the course of her pregnancy and ends up bonding with the husband over the course of her visits. While the wife seems very excited and ready to become a parent, the husband becomes increasingly more reluctant, with his feelings of not actually getting to live his dreams becoming much more obvious. His bonding with Juno makes him question whether or not he wants the life he is living.

Juno was going through her own problems, largely because of her changing hormones. She had asked that she and Paulie keep a distance between them, but when he asks someone else to prom, she gets angry and confronts him about it. He reminds her that she was the one who wanted distance and that her decision to put some space between them broke his heart. During this time, her father and stepmother are incredibly supportive, giving her some tough love and touching moments as she navigates an extremely difficult situation. Most of the film is shown through her eyes, and she narrates her thoughts, some of which are very blunt.

It was one of three movies that discussed unplanned pregnancies by unmarried women, and it got lumped in with the other two. However, it differed from the comedy *Knocked Up* and the drama *Waitress*. It became a political lightning rod for several hot-button topics, but people who watched the movie and paid attention to the characters and how the story develops dismissed the labels that some people placed on it. The point of *Juno* was more about the hard decision of a teenage girl and the way people around her reacted to her situation. At every point in time, she had choices that she could make, up to the time of the child's birth when she could have decided to keep the baby. With so much going wrong toward the end, she still managed to give up the baby to the wife because Juno felt that the wife would be a much better mother, despite the wife's situation changing. Juno is a much more complicated character than most other teenage girls depicted in the film, and it is her strong personality and focus on doing the right thing that makes her compelling to watch. Her interesting turn of phrase and the way she reacts to those around her shows that she isn't willing to simply put up with people disrespecting her or using her as an excuse. She can also recognize her flaws and when she does wrong, which is quite refreshing with a movie character, even if it takes a while to reach this point.

The movie was well received, with the responses to it being largely positive. It first showed at the Telluride Film Festival in 2007, then at the Toronto International Film Festival. Since Page and Cera are both Canadian, it makes sense that there was a major filming in their native land. The film was given a standing ovation in Toronto but was equally popular at many other festivals where it was shown over the next year. It quickly became a sensation, gaining a lot of nominations and awards. Because of the amount of buzz the movie earned because of the film circuits, its larger release date was moved up to make the most of the movie's positive reception. It was released to LA, and New York early, then was released to a few other locations across the US about a week later, then finally, it was given a wide release around Christmas 2007. Today, it has a 94% on Rotten Tomatoes and 81% on Metacritic. It won the Oscar for *Best Original Screenplay* and numerous awards across many different awards ceremonies across the film industry in many nations. Page received a lot of recognition for the portrayal of Juno because he brought the character to life in a way that felt more realistic and relatable than the character could have been if played by someone else. Page had an ease and method of delivery that made the character feel fleshed out instead of like a caricature of a pregnant teenager.

This movie was responsible for Page becoming recognizable to a much wider audience. It opened the door for Page to take on many more roles, and he was in demand in a way that most actors never achieve. Despite this, some of the issues Page faced when he was younger were becoming more obvious. There was more pressure to put on a certain type of appearance and act in a certain way that decidedly did not match how he saw himself. One of the few saving graces during this time was that he had gotten roles far outside the usual realm of teenage female actors, so Page likely did not get the kinds of roles that would require a more feminine presentation in the films. Both Hayley and Juno were more androgynous, despite Juno being pregnant, because the characters were meant to be individuals instead of stereotypes. Still, that didn't save Page on the red carpet or from expectations outside of films. That started wearing on him over the next few years.

CHAPTER 5

Needing a Break

The reception of Juno ensured that Page had at least an immediate future in acting, a future that would likely be both exciting and daunting. This was magnified by the growing disparity between how he was viewed and how he felt. Yet, at the time, it was still risky for celebrities to come out as gay, let alone transgender.

True to the kinds of roles he had taken up to that point, Page took on another role outside the typical teenage girl role in the movie *Whip It.* He took on the character of Bliss Cavendar, a 17-year-old who lived outside of Austin, Texas. Her mother is convinced that the only happiness for a young girl is to do well in beauty pageants. Under the belief that this is the key to her daughter's happiness, she pressures her reserved daughter to participate in the pageantry. Unfortunately, Bliss is not well suited for the life her mother wants her to live; she wants a life better suited to her own personality and interests. She works as a waitress and is friends with one of the other staff members named Pash. When Bliss learns of a women's roller derby league in the nearby city, she decides it is a potential path for her interests. Although she has never participated in anything like that before, Bliss proves that she has a natural talent by earning a spot on the team because of her remarkable speed on rollerblades. That's when the real problems begin – she doesn't have the killer instincts to give her an edge over others on the rink. Throughout the movie, she learns to become tougher against the competition, focusing as much on the players as on her own speed. Her other significant problem is that her parents have no idea she has joined a team and practices with them twice a week.

Much of the movie is about her attempts to keep her activities from her family. At the same time, she experiences her first crush on a musician whom she meets during one of her events. There is one more major issue that Bliss is hiding – she's underage and should not have been allowed onto a team. She had lied to be on the team, so she is also maintaining a lie with her teammates. The movie sees all of these come to a head over the last half of the film.

This could have been an ideal role for Page at the time as the growing dysmorphia between his body and his identity was likely growing because of the pressure to be more feminine while promoting movies and his career. He was similarly hiding his identity from others as he tried to find his footing. Though the movie was generally given positive reviews (with 85% on Rotten Tomatoes), more people saw it because of Page and not for the movie itself. This was Page's first financially unsuccessful Hollywood film, unlike his first two movies.

By this point, Page was feeling some of the stress and pressure that comes with growing fame, leading to him deciding to step back from work and pursue other interests for a while. This led to the actor joining an ec0-village located in Oregon. It was an eye-opening experience as the group lived a very rustic life over the course of the month that he was there. The village didn't have indoor plumbing or many other luxuries that we take for granted. The group composted virtually everything, including their own waste. Upon his arrival, Page knew no one, but living under those conditions, people learn who they are. Page said of the experience, "When I left and everyone in the class was holding hands in a circle, I was fully sobbing. One of those kinds of cries where you're just ... I would not have anticipated that's what my response would have been."

One person there also struck a chord in Page's life, Ian Danial, with Page even describing him as his "soul twin." It shows that when allowed to act far from the norm, Page found a way of living that was much more aligned with how he felt about himself.

Male or female was irrelevant – people lived the same way regardless of gender. There wasn't the kind of pressure to look or act in a certain way based on gender, just based on circumstances.

However, Page's career was back in Hollywood, and this time there was an exceptional role on the horizon—a chance to work with one of the biggest directors in a movie.

CHAPTER 6

Inception

By 2009, Christopher Nolan was a well-respected director, largely because of his dedication to his craft. The release and reception of The Dark Knight, one of the most successful releases of a comic book-based movie of the time (and is still regarded as one of the best movies, comic book or not), he had gone from someone who made intriguing and thought-provoking films to standout films that grabbed the audience's attention. Following the release of that movie and its enormous success, both commercially and critically, audiences began to go back and appreciate his earlier works. His next movie was highly anticipated because of his earlier successes. Behind the scenes, he was one of the directors most actors wanted to work with. This is why his next movie drew the attention of one of the biggest actors of the time, Leonardo DiCaprio, as well as the reliable and experienced Marion Cotillard, Ken Watanabe, and Michael Caine. Most of the cast was rounded out by many up-and-coming talents who had proven that they had some exceptional talent in the industry, including Joseph Gordon-Levitt, Tom Hardy, and Cillian Murphy. Apart from the role of DiCaprio's character's wife, played by Cotillard, there was only one other major female role, and Page managed to snag that one, fitting in nicely with the other newer talents. When asked about having such an opportunity, Page talked about how he had felt the same compulsion to be in the film as he had with Juno, "I was looking around, and the idea of this film came up and I was absolutely excited to learn more. So, I went into an office at Warner Bros. to read the script, and it was just one of those moments where you are absolutely floored."

While it was an amazing opportunity that could further show the actor's range as more than just a teenage girl fighting through troubles, *Inception* was a psychological movie that pushed the boundaries of what most audiences could comprehend. Page took on the role meant to mirror how the audience felt. Initially, his character was scouted by DiCaprio's character to join in what is best described as a reverse heist that would take place in someone's head. He introduced her to a few new concepts, but it was Gordon-Levitt's character who walked Page's character through many of the more complicated concepts that pushed the boundaries of what

Page's character had learned in college courses. The audience follows Page through the explanations, and the questions his character asks are meant to reflect the kinds of questions that the audience has. This meant the audience had a different connection to Page for much of the movie than the other actors. They also took on a similar opinion to the other characters based on how Page's character reacted to or understood those other characters.

Inception was incredibly well-received, and it remains a movie that is often a part of discussion and arguments, with people disagreeing about just what the end of the movie means. This is a common way for Nolan to end his movies, with a lot still up in the air. He tends to be less interested in answering questions and more interested in exploring characters' motives and ideas.

The experience was a double-edged sword for Page. In terms of career experience, it could not have been better for the young Page. He has been effusive with his praise for the experience, with nothing but good things to say about working with DiCaprio, whom Page had admired for years. When asked about the director, he was equally positive, replying, "I'm just constantly blown away by all his films. Despite the visual magnitude, and all the incredible action, there's this incredibly sincere base and this honesty that everything is centered around."

For Page, this was a significant point in his life

where his physical body and identity started to clash in a way they hadn't before. While there had been some dysmorphia to this point, none of the other movies had received the kind of attention or made the demands that such a major blockbuster, like *Inception*, required of the actors. *Hard Candy* was more of a study and not a dark mindset for a niche audience, and it was an indie film. *Juno* was another indie film that was seen as more of a look at a quirky teenager who navigated a very difficult situation. *Whip It* was directed by the well-known Drew Barrymore, but it was still more of an indie film because it was not a subject matter that many people found as interesting as the two earlier concepts. His fourth major movie was one of the decade's biggest movies, putting a much bigger spotlight on everyone involved. This would be an incredibly trying experience for someone dealing with internal dissonance. Unable to handle the attention and pressure to be someone he did not feel he was, Page suffered a blackout at one of the premiere after-parties. It was not the first time he had been forced to wear dresses, nor was it the first time his outwardly appearing female appearance meant being treated differently. During the premiere of *Juno*, Page picked out a suit but was told that it was not acceptable. He was then taken to stores and was required to buy a dress to wear at the last minute. His costar, Cera, hadn't even shown up in a suit, opting to wear sneakers and slacks. The males were allowed to be far more casual, while women were forced into attire they didn't always want to wear. It was disrespectful to Page because his chosen clothing was far better suited to a premiere than the casual clothing allowed to pass without a word from anyone. And it was based solely on Cera being a young male.

The difference this time was that the pressure was much more significant because *Inception* was a much bigger movie. Nor was pressure just from the studio but from the media. There is a very different expectation for young women on the red carpet than for young men, and this was starting to have a detrimental effect on Page's mental health.

CHAPTER 7

Behind the Scenes

B etween his breakout role in Hard Candy and the major film Inception, Page had roles in a few other films and documentaries, although they did not receive nearly as much attention. Following the difficulty he faced after the Inception premiers, Page appeared more interested in taking on much lower profile roles, which meant there would be less pressure for him to meet certain gender standards.

One of the exceptions to this was the role of Kitty Pryde, a minor role in the comic book movie *X-Men: The Last Stand*. The film was released in 2006, between Page's roles in *Hard Candy* and *Juno*, so he was not as well-known when the film was released. During this time, he was 18 years old and working with director Brett Ratner. According to Page, working with him was an incredibly negative experience because of the way he treated the young actor. Page was already aware that he was attracted to women, but this was not broadcasted, given how people in the LGBTQ+ community are treated in Hollywood. In addition, his career was still young, and coming out would likely have stifled his ability to get the roles he wanted.

Page did come out as gay in 2014, several years after the negative experience of working with Rattner. However, when talking about it, Page had not yet come out as trans, so during interviews addressing sexual preference, this aspect continued to be excluded from the discussion. For example, when talking about that period in his life, Page said, "I was a young adult who had not yet come out to myself. I knew I was gay, but did not know, so to speak. I felt violated when this happened.

This treatment of a young adult likely had some long-term psychological effects that made it more difficult to come to terms with who he was and slowed down the process. Instead of being able to come to his own conclusions, Page found himself in a cycle of shame and guilt; "This public, aggressive outing left me with long-standing feelings of shame, one of the most destructive results of homophobia... Ratner's comment replayed in my mind many times over the years as I encountered homophobia and coped with feelings of reluctance and uncertainty and the industry and my future in it." The outing also may have complicated

Page coming to a more powerful understanding of himself because he focused more on how people viewed him instead of better understanding himself. The focus moved more to trying to protect himself and his career, which would have been very difficult as he was still coming to terms with just a part of who he was.

Coming out in 2014 seems to have gone a long way in helping Page feel more comfortable, although it does seem to have caused a slowing in his career. When he finally came out as a lesbian, it coincided with the release of *X-Men: Days of Future Past*. He has not had another major motion role since this one, although that does not seem to be his focus anymore, perhaps because of how women are treated and because he continued to identify as a woman for the rest of the 2010s. During the *#MeToo Movement*, Page had more stories to tell of the inappropriate behavior he faced because he was perceived as female, even when he was still legally underaged.

CHAPTER 8

Coming Out

When Page finally did decide to come out, he took an approach that better aligned with the person he was becoming. During a Human Rights Campaign event, he gave a speech in which he finally said he was gay. However, the point that Page wanted to make wasn't so much about his sexual orientation but about the toxic culture in Hollywood. He spoke sincerely about how people who identified as a part of the LGBT + community were often pushed to the margins, which made him remain silent for so long. Page made it a point to highlight that it shouldn't be a choice between being who they are and having a career. This is far from a new issue in Hollywood, with some of the biggest stars in the Golden Age being members of this community, such as Rock Hudson. Studies have shown that it is damaging to a person's mental health to spend a lot of time hiding significant elements of who they are. Any large secret can be detrimental, but a person's sexuality is one of the bigger issues since it is a problem that most people within the community have faced. Another example of people trying to hide themselves is those with a disability. For example, Michael J. Fox initially hid his diagnosis of Parkinson's Disease. They did this in part so that they would be able to keep working because disclosing the conditions would have almost certainly meant that they would not be given more roles. However, the number of people who identify as part of the LGBT+ community are not only a larger community but are more often discriminated against because of it. They face a lot of online abuse and threats because of their sexual orientation. As Page said during his coming out speech, "...I am here today because I am gay. And because maybe I can make a difference." Wanting to highlight the issue, he became an advocate for the community and sought to help change the way people perceived people within the community, not just celebrities but anyone who came out.

Up to that point in time, he would say that it was the most nerve-wracking thing he had ever experienced because it was done so openly and publicly. There had already been many examples of what happened to actors who came out, and he knew he was facing a similar fate if people decided to take the same approach. Despite this, he would say of the experience, "I was just so ready to do it, and quite frankly so excited to do it, so it was a combination of just such a thrill to finally be at that place in my life where I was able to do that."

With a bigger part of him out in the open, Page began to live a much more honest life, which meant some changes to his career. With her best friend, Ian Daniel, he decided to be in a documentary where they traveled around the world as two openly gay people. Called *Gaycation*, the documentary spanned 2016 and 2017 as the pair saw what it was like to be gay all around the world. When talking about his decision to join the project, Page said, "We wanted to give a voice to those who don't always get to share their perspective or what they're going through. I think a lot of people just don't understand the difficulties a lot of people face in the community, including in America still, despite all the incredible progress." By potentially subjecting himself to some dangerous situations, Page was showing just how far he was willing to go to help make it clear just what it was like to be gay, even in places that considered themselves to be more open-minded. After all, Hollywood often purports itself to be more open-minded, but so much evidence suggests that change has been incredibly slow.

The *#MeToo Movement* was far from the first time women tried to highlight issues women faced in the industry. The previous push for change to better support women occurred during the 1990s, yet many of the highlighted issues proved to be very much still an issue. The LGBT+ community is another group of people who face challenges because of who they are. Page has spoken both for women in the industry and LGBT+ people, so he has consistently tried to make people more aware of conditions. The documentary was just one of the earliest examples of how far his support went. And for the most part, it seems to have been a largely positive experience. He and Daniel met people worldwide and saw how people started to accept who they were. While in Japan, they were present when a boy decided to tell his mother he was gay. Not all of their time was positive, though, with one of the most troubling examples being a cop who lived in Brazil and would take payments to kill gay people in the country. It was eye-opening just how people reacted to gay people, and Page reflected on how different the experience was for people in the community based on where they lived. There was a significant danger of being gay in a place like Brazil, where the police were so corrupt that they were willing to be hitmen. There are also cultural taboos in many places, with many different justifications for a bias against them. All of these would mean that there wasn't a universal experience of being gay, but there was an inherent risk of coming out nearly everywhere. The difference was what kind of risk a person would face, from losing a job to being alienated from family to being murdered.

After reflecting on this and coming to a better understanding of how fragile life is (something that most people face, just usually when they are a bit older), Page decided to make another significant change. He had become enamored of a Canadian dancer named Emma Portner, later saying, "I thought, damn, this girl is so talented and so cool. I knew right away we were both creative spirits." The couple tied the knot in 2018 and seemed very much in love in the early days. However, their careers meant they spent a lot of time apart, which tends to cause problems and rifts in relationships. They separated in 2020, around the time of Page's next big announcement, and they divorced in 2021. They still seemed to care for each other, but the nature of the relationship shifted, likely because of several reasons. Divorce rarely has a single cause but is a result of people growing apart and having a growing list of grievances and differences that can't be bridged. However, the fact that they still care shows a level of maturity and care that means they remain friends, which speaks well for both of them.

CHAPTER 9

Transitioning

Six years after coming out as gay, Page took an even larger step that seemed to have been something that he had been working toward his entire life. On Instagram, he relayed a long announcement: "Hi friends, I want to share with you that I am trans, my pronouns are he/they and my name is Elliot. I feel lucky to be writing this. To be here. To have arrived at this place in my life. I feel overwhelming gratitude for the incredible people who have supported me along this journey. I can't begin to express how remarkable it feels to finally love who I am enough to pursue my authentic self. I've been endlessly inspired by so many in the trans community. Thank you for your courage, your generosity and ceaselessly working to make this world a more inclusive and compassionate place. I will offer whatever support I can and continue to strive for a more loving and equal society." He ended the announcement with recognition of his own privilege, "To all trans people who deal with harassment, self-loathing, abuse and the threat of violence every day: I see you, I love you and I will do everything I can to change this world for the better."

The outpouring of support was swift, including from his then-wife, who posted about the subject, "I am so proud of @elliotpage. Trans, queer and non-binary people are a gift to this world. I also ask for patience & privacy but that you join me in the fervent support of trans life every single day. Elliot's existence is a gift in and of itself." Though it was not known at the time, the couple had already split up when Page made the statement, showing that it was an amicable split.

Page began to undergo surgery and other changes so that his body would align with who he was. He went on Oprah Winfrey to talk about how it has been life-changing to feel more like the embodiment of who he was instead of the misalignment between himself and his body. Following some of the initial changes, he said that he didn't feel the kind of anxiety that came from looking in the mirror, saying it was a feeling of "Oh, *there* I am." The dysmorphia began as far back as ten years old for Page, at least the memories of not feeling that his body reflected who he was. After spending about two decades feeling uncomfortable in his body, he told Oprah, "I want people to know that not only has it been life-changing for me, I believe it is life-saving and it's the case for so many people."

Again, he received a large influx of support and praise for his announcement, but there was also the expected hate and vitriol that comes with people announcing a personal choice to transition. It was this kind of hate that has helped him to remember just why he is such a strong advocate for transgender rights.

Page's life has changed since he announced his transition, and he has taken several topless photos post-operation to show off the boy that he finds much more comfortable for him. However, what most people noticed wasn't the scars, but the six-pack he sports, another significant change he's made since starting the transition. Once his body was more comfortable, he started to take better care of it. He hadn't been particularly happy with exercising in baggy clothing that he wore prior to the transition. Exercise became much more appealing, and Page would admit when talking to the magazine *Esquire*, "I'm absolutely hooked. The feeling of being really engaged with it, present, pushing it and getting stronger and gaining weight. It's thrilling."

CHAPTER 10

Awards and Accolades

P age had begun work on Umbrella Academy before announcing his transition. The first two seasons had wrapped by the time of his announcement, which could have been detrimental considering he played a female character who was instrumental in the Netflix show. Instead of ending the show or forcing Page to continue as a female character, the show incorporated the transition into the show, having the character follow a similar life trajectory. Considering all of the characters are misfits with superpowers, and his character Vanya Hargreeves making a transition into Viktor Hargreeves made sense. The outcast kids had spent their youth being manipulated by the man who adopted them, and Vanya was the only one who apparently didn't have abilities. Later, it becomes clear that Vanya did have powers, but their adoptive father could not control her and how she used her powers, so he used one of her siblings to convince Vanya that she was powerless. This meant that even within a family of misfits, Vanya was different. The correlation between Vanya and Ellen Page was very clear when considered from this angle, so having Vanya transition to Viktor the way Ellen had transitioned to Elliot seemed like a natural progression for the character. It also showed that the people behind the successful streaming show were more than willing to work with a talented young actor because he brought so much talent to the show. This was a big relief to Page because much of his time in Hollywood was spent in film. TV and streaming shows offer not only longevity and guaranteed work but it provides a much better look at characters. Movies are filmed over a shorter period of time, and there is very little room for character growth. Shows require a much greater time commitment, but actors get a chance to explore characters and backstories. Given Page started in TV, this was more of a return to his early works, and he seemed to enjoy the process: "I love watching the growth happen alongside the show, our personalities interweaving and all of us having our own moments. I'm just learning to love the whole journey of it." This is a common sentiment that people working on longer-lived shows have discussed over the years, with them often speaking of it as more of a familial experience. For shows that run for five or more years, the shows always cover substantial parts of people's lives, so this helps the cast bond in a way that doesn't exist in film.

Since 2019, Page has only appeared in two movie-length documentaries; his other work has been on shows, indicating what direction he plans to take in the future. However, it's also possible that he's more interested in working more behind the scenes. This is a likely move as he launched Page Boy Productions in 2021 and currently has a deal with Universal's UCP to work on projects for the foreseeable future. The first movie the production plans to release was announced in 2022 and is called *Backspot*.

In early 2023, Page moved in another interesting direction when he became the face of a campaign for Gucci's Guilty fragrance. He is one of three people acting as the fragrance's face during the campaign. He had always been interested in scents, even talking about how he loved how his first real boyfriend smelled when they cuddled. He now feels that scent is just as much a part of who a person is, and the way Guilty smells is something that he feels drawn to, making it easy to become one of the faces of the company.

CONCLUSION

Page has experienced significant bumps in his acting career, despite knowing that was the career he wanted from a very young age. However, he proved that no matter the odds, he was willing to find solutions to reach his goals. It didn't take long before he proved how adept he was at the craft. However, his move to California was not entirely positive, and he soon realized just how much more of a challenge it was for a woman in the industry. Between his outward appearance and how women were treated, Page had a lot of obstacles to overcome. First, he had to overcome his inappropriate behavior toward women, a gender that he didn't feel was correct for himself. At the time, the treatment likely overshadowed the dysmorphia because it put him in a more defensive position. Unfortunately, the more prominent he became as an actor, the worse the expectations became for him to conform to the expectations put on women. While his recognition as an actor helped to reduce this kind of mistreatment, it amplified the dissidence between his body and his identity.

Having experienced a wide range of negative experiences, first as a woman, then as a lesbian, and finally as a transgender male, Page has decided to use his celebrity status to help others who have suffered similar experiences. On the face of it, this seems to have meant his star has diminished because he has not been nearly so high profile since the release of *Inception*, at least not to a wider audience. He has continued to work, though, just more toward his own passion projects, and he is taking his career in a new direction which only means he can be a more vocal advocate for the LGBT+ community. Recognizing how fortunate he has been and how luck has played a large role in his success and ability to live more freely, Page has looked for ways to be more supportive. He remains a very gifted actor, and should he choose to spend more time in front of the camera beyond *Umbrella Academy*, it would be a real pleasure to see him take on more roles.

Made in the USA
Middletown, DE
28 June 2023

34051710R00031